THE BASICS OF
HIPAA
COMPLIANCE

A TRAINING MANUAL FOR EMPLOYEES

CONTENTS

Why was HIPAA Created?

The Health Insurance Portability and Accountability Act (HIPAA) was created primarily to modernize the flow of healthcare information, stipulate how Personally Identifiable Information maintained by the healthcare and healthcare insurance industries should be protected from fraud and theft, and to address limitations on healthcare insurance coverage – such as portability and the coverage of individuals with pre-existing conditions.

Although responsible for widespread changes in the healthcare and healthcare insurance industries, the changes did not occur overnight. When the Act was passed in 1996, it only required the Secretary of Health and Human Services (HSS) to propose standards that would protect individually identifiable health information. The first set of proposed "Code Set" standards was not published until 1999, and the first proposals for the Privacy Rule only emerged in 2000.

HIPAA legislation has evolved significantly since its earliest incarnation. Not only has the language of the Act been modified to address advances in technology, but the scope of the Act has been extended to cover Business Associates – third party service providers that perform a function on behalf of a HIPAA-Covered Entity that involves the use or disclosure of Protected Health Information (PHI).

The HIPAA regulations are policed by the U.S. Department of Health & Human Services' Office for Civil Rights (OCR). State Attorneys General can also take action against Covered Entities and Business Associates found not to be in compliance with HIPAA. Both OCR and State Attorneys General have the authority to impose financial penalties on Covered Entities and Business Associates for violations of HIPAA.

What is the Purpose of HIPAA?

In addition to the original purpose of HIPAA, the way in which it is implemented is constantly changing to accommodate advances in technology and changes to working practices – both of which have resulted in new threats to patient privacy and the security of PHI. For example, the original HIPAA legislation was drafted eight years before Facebook came into existence and eleven years before the first iPhone was released.

Therefore, since the original Privacy Rule, there have been a number of new HIPAA Rules (expanded on in the "HIPAA Rules Explained" section below) plus frequent guidance has been issued by OCR regarding how Covered Entities and Business Associates should address issues such as BYOD policies, cloud computing and Workplace Wellness Programs. OCR guidance has also gone digital with the release of the Listserv application.

HIPAA FACTS WORTH NOTING

◇ 1 in 7 healthcare organizations have still not designated a HIPAA Compliance Officer.

◇ 1 in 4 HIPAA breaches still go unreported.

◇ 50% of healthcare organizations believe they would fail a HIPAA Audit.

◇ 80% of healthcare organizations fail Meaningful Use audits.

◇ Unauthorized access to records accounts for 20% of HIPAA breaches.

◇ Nearly 200 million patient records were compromised between the introduction of HIPAA and 2018.

◇ About 600 HIPAA violations had been referred to the DoJ for further action by 2018.

◇ The average cost per record is $363.

◇ Phishing and Ransomware account for the vast majority of breaches by hackers.

Much of the original language of HIPAA has remained unaltered because, despite the changing technological landscape, it was written to cover a great number of diverse scenarios. Therefore, whether a Covered Entity is a medical center maintaining patient records or an insurance company transferring the healthcare rights of an individual who is changing jobs, the purpose of HIPAA remains the same as it did in 1996.

HIPAA is also technology-neutral and does not favor one way of addressing a security vulnerability over another, provided the mechanism introduced to correct a flaw or vulnerability is subjected to a risk assessment and the reason for implementing it in place of a specified measure is recorded. It is also important to note that HIPAA does not preempt state law, except in circumstances when a state's privacy and security regulations are weaker than those in HIPAA.

Understanding HIPAA

For the benefit of clarification, we have detailed below the eighteen personal identifiers that could allow a person to be identified. In the context of HIPAA, when these personal identifiers are combined with health data the information is known as "Protected Health Information" or "PHI". When stored or communicated electronically, the acronym "PHI" is preceded by an "e" – i.e. "ePHI".

Personal Identifiers

Names or part of names	Any other unique identifying characteristic
Geographical identifiers	Dates directly related to a person
Phone number details	Fax number details
Details of Email addresses	Social Security details
Medical record numbers	Health insurance beneficiary numbers
Account details	Certificate or license numbers
Vehicle license plate details	Device identifiers and serial numbers
Website URLs	IP address details
Fingerprints, retinal and voice prints	Complete face or any comparable photographic images

The main takeaway for HIPAA compliance is that any company or individual that comes into contact with PHI must enact and enforce appropriate policies, procedures and safeguards to protect data. HIPAA violations occur when there has been a failure to enact and enforce appropriate policies, procedures and safeguards, even when PHI has not been disclosed to or accessed by an unauthorized individual.

Violations of HIPAA often result from the following:

- Lack of adequate risk analyses.

- Lack of comprehensive employee training.

- Inadequate Business Associate Agreements.

- Inappropriate disclosures of PHI.

- Ignorance of the minimum necessary rule.

- Failure to report breaches within the prescribed timeframe.

Some HIPAA violations are accidental offences – for example, leaving a document containing PHI on a desk in clear view of anyone passing by. However, OCR does not consider ignorance an adequate excuse for HIPAA violations; and, although OCR may refrain from imposing a significant financial penalty on a Covered Entity for an accidental offence if the violation has not resulted in the unauthorized disclosure of PHI, it is likely that a course of "corrective action" will be required.

Who does HIPAA apply to?

Before trying to explain the ins and outs of HIPAA it is best to state when the legislation applies. Practically all health plans, healthcare clearinghouses, healthcare providers and endorsed sponsors of the Medicare prescription drug discount card are considered to be "HIPAA Covered Entities"

(CEs) under the Act. Normally, these are entities that come into contact with PHI on a constant basis.

Under the definition of HIPAA Covered Entities provided by HHS, most employers are not considered to be CEs, even if they maintain records of employees' health information. If employers use schemes such as the Employee Assistance Program (EAP), they are then considered "hybrid entities" and are required to be HIPAA-compliant.

"Business Associates" (BA) are also covered by HIPAA. These are entities who do not create, receive, manage or transmit PHI in the course of their main operations, but who supply services and perform certain functions for Covered Entities, during which they have access to PHI. Before undertaking a service or activity on behalf of a CE, a BA must complete a Business Associate Agreement guaranteeing to maintain the integrity of any PHI to which it has access, implement safeguards to protect the information, and restrict uses and disclosures of the information.

HIPAA Rules Explained

HIPAA legislation is essentially comprised of a number of rules, each of which lays out different requirements for HIPAA compliance. The rules are as follows:

FIVE KEY HIPAA RULES

HIPAA Privacy Rule
Governs PHI Disclosure

HIPAA Security Rule
Standards to Safeguard ePHI

Omnibus Rule
Merges HITECH Rules into HIPAA

Breach Notification Rule
Steps Required After a Breach of Security

Enforcement Rule
Governs How Investigations are Conducted

HIPAA Privacy Rule

The Privacy Rule dictates how, when and under what circumstances PHI can be used and disclosed. Enacted for the first time in 2003, it applies to all healthcare organizations, clearinghouses and entities that provide health plans. Since 2013, it has been extended to include Business Associates.

The Privacy Rule sets limits regarding the use of patient information when no prior authorization has been given by the patient. Additionally, it mandates patients and their representatives have the right to obtain a copy of their health records and request corrections to errors. CEs have a 30-day deadline to respond to such requests.

HIPAA Security Rule

The Security Rule sets the minimum standards to safeguard ePHI. Anybody within a CE or BA who can access, create, alter or transfer ePHI must follow these standards. Technical safeguards include encryption to NIST standards if the data goes outside the company's firewall.

Physical safeguards may relate to the layout of workstations (e.g. screens cannot be seen from a public area), whereas administrative safeguards unite the Privacy Rule and the Security Rule. They require a Security Officer and Privacy Officer to conduct regular risk assessments and audits. These assessments aim to identify any ways in which the integrity of PHI is threatened and build a risk management policy off the back of this.

Breach Notification Rule

The Department of Health and Human Services must be notified if a data breach has been discovered. This must be within 60 days of the breach's discovery for incidents involving 500 or more individuals, and within 60 days of the end of the calendar year in which the breach was experienced for breaches of fewer than 500 records. Individuals whose personal information has been compromised must also be informed within 60 days, and if more than five hundred patients are affected in a particular jurisdiction, a media notice must be issued to a prominent news outlet serving that area.

Omnibus Rule

The Omnibus Rule activated HIPAA-related changes that had been part of the HITECH Act. These included the extension of HIPAA coverage to BAs, the prohibition of using PHI for marketing or fundraising purposes without authorization and new penalty tiers for violations of HIPAA. Part of those penalties can be retained by OCR to fund more stringent investigations of data breaches and complaints of noncompliance.

Enforcement Rule

Should a breach of PHI occur, this rule lays out how any resulting investigations are carried out. Once the level of negligence has been determined, appropriate fines can be issued. For example, if it is determined that the violation was due to ignorance, a fine of up to $50,000 can be levied against the negligent party per violation with an annual maximum of $25,000 for violations of an identical provision. If the violation was because of willful neglect and was not rectified within 30 days, a fine of $50,000 per offence is possible up to an annual maximum of $1,500,000 for violations of an identical provision.

Since the Final Omnibus Rule was introduced in 2013, new guidelines have been released on how PHI must be accessed and sent in a medical-related environment. The revised Act allocates patients further rights to know and manage how their health information is used.

HIPAA-covered entities and Business Associates must put in place mechanisms to limit the flow of information inside a private network, monitor activity on the network and take steps to stop the unauthorized disclosure of PHI beyond the network's boundaries. More attention must be invested in conducting risk assessments, and new reporting procedures have been implemented to cover data breaches.

Changes to the HIPAA Security Rule list the conditions ("safeguards") that must be in place for HIPAA-compliant storage and the communication of ePHI. These "safeguards" are referred to in the HIPAA Security Rule as either "required" or "addressable". In fact, all the security measures are generally required – irrespective of how they are listed – as the following section explains.

The Required and Addressable Security Measures of HIPAA Explained

One area of HIPAA that has resulted in some confusion is the difference between "required" and "addressable" security measures. Practically every safeguard of HIPAA is "required" unless there is a justifiable rationale not to implement the safeguard, or an appropriate alternative to the safeguard is put in place that achieves the same objective and provides an equivalent level of protection.

An instance in which the implementation of an addressable safeguard might be not required is the encryption of email. Emails containing ePHI – either in the body or as an attachment – only have to be encrypted if they are shared beyond a firewalled, internal server. If a healthcare group only uses email as an internal form of communication – or has an authorization from a patient to send their information unencrypted outside the protection of the firewall – there is no need to adopt this addressable safeguard.

The decision not to use email encryption will have to be backed up by a risk assessment and must be documented in writing. Other factors that may have to be considered are the organization's risk mitigation strategy and other security measures put in place to secure the integrity of PHI. As a footnote to this particular section of HIPAA explained, the encryption of PHI at rest and in transit is recommended.

HIPAA Encryption Requirements

HIPAA-covered entities are required to implement safeguards to ensure the confidentiality, integrity, and availability of ePHI. Arguably one of the most important safeguards is encryption, especially on portable devices such as laptop computers that are frequently taken off site.

Encryption renders ePHI unreadable and undecipherable. The data can only be read if a key or code is applied to decrypt the data. If a portable device containing encrypted ePHI is stolen, and the code or key to decrypt the data is not also obtained, the data cannot be viewed.

While HIPAA was deliberately technology-agnostic, data encryption is mentioned in the HIPAA Security Rule, but it is only an addressable specification. HIPAA-covered entities must consider using encryption, but it is not mandatory for ePHI to be encrypted at rest or in transit.

HIPAA-covered entities should conduct a risk analysis and determine which safeguards are the most appropriate given the level of risk and their workflow.

If the decision is taken not to use encryption, an alternative safeguard can be used in its place, provided it is reasonable and appropriate and provides an equivalent level of protection. If encryption is not used, the decision not to encrypt must be documented along with the reasons why encryption was not used and the alternative safeguards that were used in its place.

If the decision is taken to encrypt data, HIPAA-covered entities should use an appropriate encryption standard. The National Institute of Standards and Technology (NIST) recommends Advanced Encryption Standard (AES) 128, 192 or 256-bit encryption, OpenPGP, and S/MIME – although *these standards may change*.

HIPAA Password Requirements

HIPAA is vague when it comes to specific technologies and controls that should be applied to secure ePHI and systems that store health information, and this is certainly true for passwords.

Even though passwords are one of the most basic safeguards to prevent unauthorized accessing of data and accounts, there is little mention of passwords in HIPAA. The only HIPAA password requirements that are specified are that HIPAA-covered entities and their business associates must implement "Procedures for creating, changing, and safeguarding passwords."

Even though password requirements are not detailed in HIPAA, HIPAA covered entities should develop policies covering the creation of passwords and base those policies on current best practices. It is strongly recommended that healthcare organizations follow the advice of NIST when creating password policies.

While NIST has previously recommended the use of complex passwords, its advice on passwords has recently been revised. Highly complex passwords may be 'more secure' but they are difficult to remember. As a result, employees often write their passwords down. To avoid this, passwords should be difficult to guess but also memorable. The use of long passphrases rather than passwords is now recommended.

Generally, passwords should:

- Be a minimum of 8 characters up to 64 characters, with passphrases – memorized secrets – longer than standard passwords recommended.

- NIST advises against storing password hints as these could be accessed by unauthorized individuals and be used to guess passwords.

- A password policy should be implemented to prevent commonly used weak passwords from being set, such as 'password', '12345678', 'letmein' etc.

- NIST now recommends not forcing users to change their passwords frequently. A change should only be required infrequently or if there is very good reason for doing so – such as following a security breach.

- Multi-factor authentication should be implemented.

- NIST recommends salting and hashing stored passwords using a one-way key derivation function.

HIPAA Record Retention Requirements

There are no HIPAA record retention requirements as far as medical records are concerned but medical record retention requirements are covered by state laws. Data retention policies must therefore be developed accordingly.

For instance, a hospital in the state of South Carolina must retain medical records for 11 years after the discharge date, while in Florida medical records must be retained by physicians for five years after the last patient contact and hospitals must retain medical records for seven years after the discharge date.

When medical records are retained, they must be kept secure at all times. HIPAA requires appropriate administrative, technical, and physical safeguards to be implemented to ensure the confidentiality, integrity, and availability of ePHI from the date of creation of ePHI to its secure disposal.

While there is not a minimum HIPAA medical record retention period, HIPAA does require covered entities to retain HIPAA-related documents. CFR §164.316(b)(2)(i) states that HIPAA-related documents must be retained for a period of six years from the date that the document was created. For policies, it is six years from when the policy was last in effect.

Insurance companies may be subject to FINRA laws which cover the retention of certain records. The Fair Labor Standards Act and the Employee Retirement Income Security Act also require certain records to be retained and the Centers for Medicare & Medicaid Services (CMS) requires healthcare providers to retain cost reports for five years after the closure of the cost report, while Medicare managed care program providers are required to retain records for ten years.

HIPAA Violation Reporting Requirements

The HIPAA Breach Notification Rule – 45 CFR §§ 164.400-414 – requires notifications to be issued after a breach of unsecured protected health information.

A breach is defined as a use or disclosure of protected health information not permitted by the HIPAA Privacy Rule that compromises the security or privacy of protected health information. Notifications are not required if a HIPAA-covered entity or business associate can demonstrate there is a low probability that PHI has been compromised, with that determination made through a risk analysis.

If notifications are required, they must be issued to patients/health plan members 'without unnecessary delay' and no later than 60 days after the discovery of a breach. A media notice must also be issued if the breach impacts more than 500 individuals, again within 60 days. The notice should be provided to a prominent media outlet in the state or jurisdiction where the breach victims are located.

The individual and media notices should include a brief description of the security breach, the types of information exposed, a brief description of what is being done by the breached entity to mitigate harm and prevent future breaches, and the steps that can be taken by breach victims to reduce the potential for harm.

The HHS' Secretary must also be notified within 60 days of the discovery of a breach if the breach impacts 500 or more individuals, and within 60 days of the end of the calendar year in which the breach was experienced if the breach impacts fewer than 500 individuals.

A copy of the breach notices should be retained along with documentation showing that notifications were issued. If a security breach did not warrant the issuing of notifications, documentation must be retained detailing the risk assessment that established there was a low probability that PHI was compromised.

Most Common HIPAA Violations

A HIPAA violation is the failure to comply with any of the provisions of HIPAA Rules. While there are many potential areas where HIPAA Rules can be violated, ten of the most common HIPAA violations are detailed below. These violations have been discovered by OCR during investigations of data breaches and complaints filed by employees, patients, and plan members through the OCR complaints portal.

COMMON CAUSES of HIPAA VIOLATIONS

◇ Unauthorized access to records

◇ Employee accidental disclosure

◇ Lost or stolen devices

◇ Employee dishonesty

◇ Insufficient IT security measures

◇ Incorrect admin procedures

◇ Business associate disclosure

◇ Professional hackers

◇ Improper disposal

Risk Analysis Failures

One of the most common HIPAA violations discovered by OCR is the failure to perform a comprehensive, organization-wide risk analysis. HIPAA requires covered entities and their business associates to conduct regular risk analyses to identify vulnerabilities to the confidentiality, integrity, and availability of PHI.

Risk Management Failures

All risks identified during the risk analysis must be subjected to a HIPAA-compliant risk management process and reduced to a reasonable and appropriate level. Risk management is critical to the security of ePHI and PHI and is a fundamental requirement of the HIPAA Security Rule.

Lack of Encryption or Alternative Safeguards

While HIPAA does not demand the use of encryption, encryption is an addressable implementation specification and must be considered. The failure to use encryption or an alternative equivalent safeguard to ensure the confidentiality, integrity, and availability of ePHI has resulted in many healthcare data breaches.

Security Awareness Training Failures

HIPAA requires covered entities and business associates to implement a security awareness training program for all members of the workforce, including management. Training should be provided regularly and the frequency should be determined by means of a risk analysis.

Improper Disposal of PHI

When PHI or ePHI is no longer required it must be disposed of securely in a manner that ensures PHI is "unreadable, indecipherable, and otherwise cannot be reconstructed." Paper records should be shredded, burnt, pulped, or pulverized, while electronic media should be cleared, purged, degaussed, or destroyed.

Impermissible Disclosures of PHI

An impermissible disclosure of PHI is a disclosure not permitted under the HIPAA Privacy Rule. This includes providing PHI to a third party without first obtaining consent from a patient and 'disclosures' when unencrypted portable electronic devices containing ePHI are stolen.

Failure to Adhere to the Minimum Necessary Standard

Covered entities must take steps to limit access to PHI to the minimum necessary information to achieve the intended purpose.

Failure to Provide Patients with Copies of PHI on Request

The Privacy Rule permits patients to access PHI and obtain copies of their protected health information on request. Requests for copies of PHI must be dealt with promptly and copies provided within 30 days of the request being received.

Failure to Enter into A Business Associate Agreement

Healthcare organizations may require individuals or entities to provide services that require access to PHI. Prior to any disclosure of PHI, the entity that performs those functions must enter into a business associate agreement (BAA) with the covered entity. The BAA outlines the business associate's responsibilities to safeguard PHI, explains the permissible uses and disclosures of PHI, and other requirements of HIPAA.

Failure to Issue Breach Notifications Promptly

In the event of a data breach, notifications must be issued to affected individuals to alert them to the exposure of their PHI. Breach notifications must be issued without unreasonable delay and no later than 60 days from the date of discovery of the breach.

HIPAA Implications for Patients

The HIPAA implications for patients are that their healthcare information is treated more sensitively and can be accessed more quickly by their healthcare suppliers. Electronically stored health information is now better secured than paper records ever were, and healthcare groups that have put in place mechanisms to adhere with HIPAA regulations are witnessing greater efficiency. This results – as far as patients are concerned – in a higher standard of healthcare.

On the negative side, healthcare groups are not only concerned with the standard of healthcare they can give to individual patients. Healthcare groups want to increase the services they can supply, want to enhance the quality of care and improve patient safety through research. Regrettably, research is limited by HIPAA, and restricted access to PHI has the potential to slow the pace at which improvements can be made in healthcare.

There is also a price to pay for better data security, and although the enactment of the Meaningful Use program gave financial incentives for healthcare providers to digitalize paper records, adapting the necessary controls to secure ePHI can carry a substantial cost. Increasing funding for compliance may reduce the level of patient care, while the administrative strain that HIPAA-compliance places of healthcare organizations furthers exhausts available resources.

Explaining HIPAA to Patients

Healthcare organizations are now required by law to give patients a notice of their privacy practices and get patients to sign to confirm receipt of the document. A good practice to adopt is to put all relevant information in the Notice of Privacy Practices and then give patients a summary of what the policy contains. For instance, explain to the patient:

- They may request their medical records whenever they like.

- They may request you amend their medical records to correct errors.

- They can limit who has access to their personal health information.

- They can choose how you communicate with them.

- They have right to complain about the unauthorized disclosure of their PHI and suspected HIPAA violations.

Healthcare Organizations and the Implications of HIPAA

If data privacy and security is not adequately managed, the Office for Civil Rights can issue fines for non-compliance. Avoidable data breaches could see considerable financial penalties applied. Under the penalty structure brought in by HITECH Act, violations can lead to fines up to $50,000 per violation up to a maximum of $1.5 million per year, for violations of an identical provision. Lawsuits can also be initiated by state attorneys general and fines of up to $250,000 per violation category are possible. Covered entities and Business Associates may also be sued by victims of data breaches.

HIPAA VIOLATION PENALTIES

HIPAA Violation	Minimum Penalty	Maximum Penalty
Unknowing	$100 per violation, with an annual maximum of $25,000 for repeat violations (Note: maximum that can be imposed by State Attorneys General regardless of the type of violation)	$50,000 per violation, with an annual maximum of $1.5 million
Reasonable Cause	$1,000 per violation, with an annual maximum of $100,000 for repeat violations	$50,000 per violation, with an annual maximum of $1.5 million
Willful neglect but violation is corrected within the required time period	$10,000 per violation, with an annual maximum of $250,000 for repeat violations	$50,000 per violation, with an annual maximum of $1.5 million
Willful neglect and is not corrected within required time period	$50,000 per violation, with an annual maximum of $1.5 million	$50,000 per violation, with an annual maximum of $1.5 million

CEs and BAs – and their employees – who breach HIPAA for personal gain or under false pretenses can be held criminally liable and have criminal penalties imposed by the Office for Civil Rights, via the Department of Justice, which can include a fine of up to $250,000, restitution, and up to ten years' imprisonment with a further two years for aggravated identity theft.

The high odds of healthcare organizations becoming targets for cybercriminals and the exorbitant cost of addressing data breaches – issuing breach notification correspondence, offering credit monitoring services and covering regulatory fines, and legal costs – is far higher than the cost of achieving full compliance. But, while the initial investment in the necessary technical, physical and administrative security measures to secure patient data may be high, the improvements can lead to savings over time as a result of improved efficiency.

Organizations that have already implemented mechanisms to adhere with HIPAA often see their workflows streamlined and the workforce can become more productive, allowing healthcare organizations to reinvest their savings and provide a higher standard of healthcare to patients.

Explaining HIPAA to Staff

Explaining HIPAA to staff members of CEs and BAs requires far more work than explaining HIPAA to patients. In order to adhere with HIPAA, organizations must compile privacy and security policies for their employees, and develop a sanctions policy for staff members who do not comply with HIPAA requirements. Therefore it is important to explain HIPAA to workers HIPAA in greater detail.

The best method of explaining HIPAA to employees is in special compliance training tutorials. Although the HIPAA regulations require training to be provided annually, we feel there is so much for employees to take in relating to the security and privacy of personal health information, that compliance training sessions are better short and frequent. Trying to explain HIPAA to employees in a four-hour training session will likely fail.

A lot of the explanation will concentrate on the privacy and security of PHI, but how this is adopted will likely have an effect on the employees themselves. For instance, employees should be prevented from exchanging information about patient healthcare via their mobile device unless appropriate controls have been implemented. Due to the number of healthcare centers adopting BYOD policies, this will mean workers may have to download safe communication apps to their personal mobile devices in order to communicate ePHI.

Summary

In a way, HIPAA was quite forward-thinking. Although Congress had been passing privacy laws since the 1970s, HIPAA addressed the digitalization of medical records and stipulated the safeguards HIPAA-covered entities should apply in order to protect healthcare data in both paper and digital formats. The digitalization of medical records was later encouraged via amendments in the HITECH Act to bring HIPAA up to date.

Compliance with HIPAA is an ongoing exercise. There is no one-off compliance test or certification one can achieve that will absolve a Covered Entity from sanctions if an avoidable breach or violation of HIPAA subsequently occurs. Indeed, OCR has issued a statement advising Covered Entities and Business Associates that it does not endorse any private consultants' or education providers' seminars, materials or systems, nor does it certify any persons or products as "HIPAA compliant."

If you are unsure about any element of HIPAA, it is recommended you seek professional advice. It has already been mentioned above that ignorance of HIPAA is not an adequate excuse for noncompliance, and there does not necessarily need to have been an unauthorized disclosure of PHI in order for a violation of HIPAA to warrant sanctions. Therefore, although the resources required to achieve HIPAA compliance may be considerable, there is no alternative if your organization collects, processes, stores or disposes of PHI or ePHI that to become compliant with HIPAA.

GLOSSARY

Access

The ability or the means necessary to read, write, modify, or communicate data/information or otherwise make use of any system resource.

Accounting for Disclosures

Information that describes a covered entity's disclosures of PHI other than for treatment, payment and health care operations; disclosures made with authorization; and certain other limited disclosures. For those categories of disclosures that need to be in the accounting, the accounting must include disclosures that have occurred during the 6 years (or a shorter time period at the request of the individual) prior to the date of the request for an accounting.

Administrative Safeguard

Administrative actions, and policies and procedures, to manage the selection, development, implementation, and maintenance of security measures to protect electronic protected health information and to manage the conduct of the covered entity's or business associate's workforce in relation to the protection of that information.

Amendment and Correction

An amendment to a record would indicate that the data is in dispute while retaining the original information.   A correction to a record alters or replaces the original record.

Authorization

Written permission by the patient or the patient's personal representative to use and/or disclose protected health information about the individual. The requirements of a valid authorization are defined in the HIPAA regulations.

Blog

A contraction of the term weblog.   A website, usually maintained by an individual or a group of individuals with regular entries of commentary, description of events, or other material including graphics or video.

Breach

The unauthorized acquisition, access, use or disclosure of protected health information which compromises the security or privacy of such information, except where an unauthorized person to whom such information is disclosed, would not reasonably have been able to retain such information.

An impermissible use or disclosure is presumed to be a breach unless the covered entity or business associate, as applicable, demonstrates that there is a low probability that the protected health information has been compromised.

Business Associate

An individual or entity who performs certain functions or activities on behalf of IU that involve the use or disclosure of PHI. Business associate functions and activities include: claims processing or administration; data analysis, processing or administration; utilization review; quality assurance; billing; benefit management; practice management; and repricing. Business associate services are: legal; actuarial; accounting; consulting; data aggregation; management; administrative; accreditation; and financial. A covered entity may be a business associate of another covered entity.

Business Associate Agreement

A written contract between a covered entity and a business associate (BA) that establishes the permitted and required uses and disclosures of protected health information by the BA; requires the BA to implement appropriate safeguards to prevent unauthorized use or disclosure; requires BA to report to covered entity any uses and disclosures not provided for in the contract; to the extent the business associate is to carry out a covered entity's obligation under the Privacy Rule, requires the business associate to comply with the requirements applicable to the obligation; requires BA to ensure any subcontractors agree to the same restrictions.

Complaint

A statement that a situation is unsatisfactory or unacceptable; An allegation of wrongdoing against an individual or organization.

Covered Entity

A health plan, a health care clearinghouse, or a health care provider who transmits any health information in electronic form in connection with transactions covered by the HIPAA Privacy Rule.

Critical Data

Data if inappropriately handled may result in criminal or civil penalties, identity theft, personal financial loss, invasion of privacy, or unauthorized access by an individual or many individuals (e.g., student loan information, social security number, driver's license number, passport or Visa number, state ID card number and protected health information).

Data Use Agreement

An agreement required by the Privacy Rule between a covered entity (the holder of the PHI) and a person or entity that receives the limited data set (e.g. a research investigator) when the data are in the form of a limited data set. A Data use agreement establishes the ways in which the information in the limited data set may be used and how it will be protected.

De-Identified Health Information

Health information that does not identify an individual, and with respect to which there is no reasonable basis to believe that the information can be used to identify an individual.

Designated Record Set

A group of records maintained by or for a covered entity that is: the medical records and billing records about individuals maintained by or for a covered health care provider; enrollment, payment, claims adjudication, and case or medical management record systems maintained by or for a health plan; or used, in whole or in part, by or for the covered entity to make decisions about individuals.

Any item, collection, or grouping of information that includes protected health information and is maintained, collected, used, or disseminated by or for a covered entity.

Disclosure

Release, transfer, provisions of, access to, or divulgence in any manner of information outside the entity holding the information.

Electronic Protected Health Information

Protected health information (PHI) created, maintained or transmitted in electronic form (ePHI).

Encryption

The use of an algorithmic process to transform data into a form in which there is a low probability of assigning meaning without use of a confidential process or key.

Fundraising

Appeals for money, sponsorship of events, etc. for the benefit of a covered entity. HIPAA allows the disclosure of protected health information for this purpose without an individual's authorization.

Health Information Exchange (HIE)

The process of reliable and interoperable electronic health-related information sharing conducted in a manner that protects the confidentiality privacy and security of the information. The electronic movement of health-related information among organizations according to nationally recognized standards.

Health Information Exchanges (HIE)

An organization that oversees and governs the exchange of health-related information among organizations according to nationally recognized standards.

Health Information Technology for Economic and Clinical Health Act (HITECH Act)

Federal law enacted as part of the American Recovery and Reinvestment Act (ARRA) of 2009. The HITECH Act promotes adoption and meaningful use of health information technology; widens the scope of privacy and security protections available under HIPAA; increases the potential legal liability for non- compliance; and provides for more enforcement.

Health Insurance Portability and Accountability Act (HIPAA)

A Federal law that allows persons to qualify immediately for comparable health insurance coverage when they change their employment relationships. Also gives Health and Human Services (HHS) the authority to mandate the use of standards for the electronic exchange of health care data; to specify what medical and administrative code sets should be used within those standards; to require the use of national identification systems for health care patients, providers, payers (or plans), and employers (or sponsors); and to specify the types of measures required to protect the security and privacy of personally identifiable health care information.

Healthcare Operations

Certain activities of the covered entity that are related to covered functions. These activities include, but are not limited to: administrative, financial, legal, underwriting and quality improvement activities that are necessary for a covered entity to run its business.

Incidental Use and Disclosure

Secondary use[s] and disclosure[s] of protected health information (PHI) that cannot reasonably be prevented, limited in nature and that occur as a byproduct of an otherwise permitted use or disclosure.

Individual

The person who is the subject of protected health information.

Individually Identifiable Health Information (IIHI)

A subset of health information, including demographic information collected from an individual, and: (1) is created or received by a health care provider, health plan, employer, or health care clearinghouse; and (2) relates to the past, present, or future physical or mental health or condition of an individual; the provision of health care to an individual; or the past, present, or future payment for the provision of health care to an individual; and identifies the individual or there is a reasonable basis to believe the information can be used to identify the individual.

IU Fundraising

Personnel: Includes any IU employees or other IU personnel, including but not limited to the IU Office of Gift Development, who perform any fundraising activities on behalf of, or in affiliation, with another covered entity, such as the IU Health Physicians, the IU School of Medicine Clinical Departments or other HIPAA Covered Entity, and may have access to or use Protected Health Information for fundraising purposes.

IU HIPAA Affected Areas (IU HAAs)

Any school, department, division, or unit that may be a health care component; perform business associate services to another covered entity or a health care component; or have access to protected health information for education and/or research purposes.

Limited Data Set

A data set of protected health information that excludes specified direct identifiers related to an individual or of relatives, employers, or household members of the individual, but retains geographic subdivisions larger than the postal address, elements of dates including month and day as well as other unique identifying numbers, characteristics or codes not previously listed as a direct identifier and cannot reasonably be used to identify an individual. Limited data sets may only be used for research, public health or for health care operations; and only in conjunction with a data use agreement.

Malware

Short for malicious software. Software the is intended to damage or disable computers and computer systems. Malware includes computer programs known as viruses, worms, Trojans, ransomware and spyware.

Marketing

A communication about a product or service that encourages recipients of the communication to purchase or use the product or service. Using protected health information for marketing purposes requires an authorization from the patient, unless the communication is: a face-to-face communication made by a covered entity to an individual; or a promotional gift of nominal value.

Minimum Necessary

A standard that requires covered entities to take reasonable steps to limit the use or disclosure of, and requests for PHI to the minimum necessary to accomplish the intended purpose. The minimum necessary standard does not apply to certain uses or disclosures such as those requests by a health care provider for treatment purposes, disclosures to the individual who is the subject of the information or pursuant to an individual's authorization.

Mobile Computing Device or Mobile Device

A small device, typically small enough to be handheld, that is capable of collecting, storing, transmitting, or processing electronic data or images. These may include a cellular telephone, mobile phone, smart phone, PDA, non-laptop based tablet (e.g. iPad, kindle, android), or USB-device. IU includes laptop and notebook computers in its definition of "mobile device".

Notice of Privacy Practices

The Rule requires health plans and covered health care providers to provide adequate notice that provides a clear, user friendly explanation of the individual's legal rights with respect to their personal health information and the privacy practices of the covered entity.

Observer

An individual who has:

1.   Completed the forms required by this Guidance Document

2.   Been approved by a Unit: and

3.   Been assigned to a Supervisor within a Unit to shadow an employee or healthcare provider.

It is highly recommended that Observers be at least 18 years of age to do an on the job shadowing experience with a healthcare provider.

Phishing

The activity of defrauding an online account holder by posing as a legitimate company or person.

Phishing Schemes

A form of fraud in which the attacker tries to learn information such as login credentials or account information by masquerading as a reputable entity or person in email IM or other communication channels.

Physician-Patient e- mail

Computer-based communication between physicians or associated medical personnel and patients within a professional relationship in which the physician has taken on an explicit measure of responsibility for the patient's care. [844 IAC 5-1-1]

These guidelines do not apply to communication between caregivers and consumers in which no on-going professional relationship exists. E-mail communications does not include communication via social networking sites or cell phone short messaging services (texting).

Payment

Activities undertaken by a health care provider to obtain payment or be reimbursed for their services and of a health plan to obtain premiums, to fulfill their coverage responsibilities and provide benefits under the plan, and to obtain or provide reimbursement for the provision of health care.

Personally Identifiable Information (PII)

Information which can be used to distinguish or trace an individual's identity, such as their name, Social Security Number, biometric records, etc. alone, or when combined with other personal or identifying information which is linked or linkable to a specific individual, such as date and place of birth, mother's maiden name, etc. It includes information that is linked or linkable to an individual, such as medical, educational, financial and employment information.

Physical Safeguards

Physical measures, policies and procedures to protect a covered entity's paper records and electronic information systems and related building and equipment from natural and environmental hazards and unauthorized intrusion.

Protected Health Information (PHI)

Individually identifiable health information held or transmitted by a covered entity or its business associate in any form or medium, whether electronic, on paper or oral.

Recording

The action or process of storing sounds and images on electronic media or paper so they can be heard and/or seen again. Includes all methods of recording photographs, images, videos, audio and other digital or electronic media by which the identity of the recorded individual may be determined.

Safeguards

Specific actions which are designed to protect the privacy and security of an individual's health information. These actions may include: administrative measures such as policies, procedures, training and written agreements; physical measures such as locked doors or keycard access; and technical measures such as firewalls, password/passphrase and encryption.

Sanitizing electronic media

A process by which data is irreversibly removed from media or the media is permanently destroyed. It includes removing all classified labels, markings, and activity logs.

Secure Destruction

The result of actions taken to ensure that media cannot be reused as originally intended and that information is virtually impossible to recover.

Security Incident Response Team

A group of individuals created to assist with an incident investigation. The incident response team will be activated at the discretion of the Information Security Office (ISO). The core IU Health incident response team members will be decided with each incident by the ISO. This team may typically consist of General Counsel representatives, IS representatives, a Media Relations Office representative, and a Compliance Office representative.

Security Incident

The attempted or successful unauthorized access, use, disclosure, modification, or destruction of information or interference with system operations in an information system.

Site

The location where an Observer will watch an employee or Faculty member at work. The healthcare facility or practice that occupies the Site will be responsible for the administration of the shadowing experience in accordance with this policy or the facility's policy. For purposes of this policy, the term site may include but not be limited to a school clinic, department, practices, clinics or hospitals affiliated with Indiana University.

Social Networking Sites

Internet sites that provide a variety of ways for users to interact, such as e-mail instant messaging, posting informational web pages and picture exchange services. Common Internet social networking sites are Facebook, Twitter, Instagram, LinkedIn, Pinterest, Google Plus+, Tumblr, VK, Flickr, Vine and Myspace.

Social Networking

Online communities of people who share interests and/or activities, or who are interested in exploring the interests and activities of others. Most social network services are web based and provide a variety of ways for users to interact, such as e-mail instant messaging and picture exchange services.

Supervisor

An individual employed by or affiliated with the respective Health Science School or affiliated healthcare facility participating in the job shadowing experience and is responsible for determining when access to confidential information is appropriate.

Technical Safeguards

The technology and the policy and procedures for its use that protect electronic protected health information and control access to it.

Treatment

The provision, coordination, or management of health care and related services by one or more health care providers, including the coordination or management of health care by a health care provider with a third party; consultation between health care providers relating to a patient; or the referral of a patient for health care from one health care provider to another.

Use

With respect to individually identifiable health information, the sharing, employment, application, utilization, examination, or analysis of such information within an entity that maintains such information.

User

A person who uses a computer or network service. At IU this includes faculty, staff, students, affiliates, temporary workers, retired faculty, retired staff and any individuals or entities that use or have authorized access to IU's network.

Unit

A clinical or non-clinical department within one of IU's Health Science Schools.

Workforce member

Employees, volunteers, trainees (including students, residents and fellows), and other persons whose conduct, in the performance of work for a covered entity, is under the direct control of such entity, whether or not they are paid by the covered entity.

ACKNOWLEDGEMENT of RECEIPT
Basics of HIPAA Compliance — A Guide for Employees

This acknowledges that the employee has received a copy of the Company's Employee Guide to Basic HIPAA Compliance, has had the opportunity to read the Guide, discuss the Guide with management and have questions answered, and understands the content presented in the Guide. Although it reflects the Company's current Policy regarding HIPAA compliance requirements, it may be necessary to make changes from time to time to best serve the needs of the organization or comply with changes in applicable laws or regulations. Any changes deemed necessary will be made in writing, and the modified Guide will be shared with all employees.

The employee further acknowledges that annual HIPAA training is required by law and by Company policy and agrees to participate in and complete such training as may be required by the Company from time to time.

By my signature below, I acknowledge that I have received a copy of the Company's Employee Guide to Basic HIPAA Compliance. I have read, understood, and agree to comply with the procedures and provisions set forth in the Guide and to complete such HIPAA training as may be required by the Company from time to time.

_____

Date

_____

Employee's Signature

_____

Printed Name of Employee